What Happens When You Strengthen and Regulate the Teen Mind & Brain?

...You just might end up with a happier, healthier, more resilient and loving human being!

Parents are struggling like never before in human history. Age-old issues are now being compounded with new age challenges facing our teens and adolescents. So how do we break the cycle and get ahead of the game?

In this revolutionary Itty Bitty Book, Gretchen Downey gives you a preview into the amazing and hidden world of the teen mind. She'll teach you fundamental tools for understanding and navigating this incredible transformational period of your child's life.

Embracing and practicing these 15 simple yet powerful strategies will help you and your teen in immeasurable ways. Such as showing you:

- How to strengthen internal happiness and joy

- How to better regulate emotions and thoughts

- Ways to foster cooperation, value and respect

Pick up a copy of this powerful book today and start building the relationship and family life that you and your teen want!

Your Amazing Itty Bitty® Parenting Teens Book

15 Powerful Parenting Strategies for Understanding How Your Teen Thinks

Gretchen E. Downey

Published by Itty Bitty® Publishing
A subsidiary of S & P Productions, Inc.

Copyright © 2015 Gretchen E. Downey

All rights reserved. No part of this book may be reproduced or transmitted in any form or by any means, electronic or mechanical, including photocopying, recording or by any information storage and retrieval system, without written permission of the publisher, except for inclusion of brief quotations in a review.

Printed in the United States of America

Itty Bitty® Publishing
311 Main Street, Suite E
El Segundo, CA 90245
(310) 640-8885

ISBN: 978-1-931191-89-0

*This book is dedicated to misunderstood teens of the world.
~ May you soon be fully recognized and valued for the
magnificent beings that you are!*

Stop by our Itty Bitty® website to find interesting blog entries regarding teen parenting.

www.IttyBittyPublishing.com

For more information on conscious parenting topics and to obtain a copy of a comprehensive parenting guidebook that you can use for a lifetime ("Mind Body Spirit Parenting Guidebook – Developing the Conscious Child"), visit my website at:

www.thekidwhisper.com

Table of Contents

Strategy 1.	Where Did My Kid Go? Understanding The Great Brain Migration
Strategy 2.	Erasing the Misery of Myths
Strategy 3.	Words – The Weapon of The Wise
Strategy 4.	Leave Me Alone!
Strategy 5.	There's a New Family in Town - Peers
Strategy 6.	You Are Not Your Emotions
Strategy 7.	Novelty! Novelty! Novelty!
Strategy 8.	From Limitations to Limitlessness
Strategy 9.	Building Mindful Awareness
Strategy 10.	Body Alignment
Strategy 11.	Discipline Done Right
Strategy 12.	Leverage Your "Wrongs"
Strategy 13.	Banishing Beliefs
Strategy 14.	Selective Parenting
Strategy 15.	The Happiness Factor

Introduction

Science is revealing new ways of looking at the adolescent brain, specifically during the period between approximately twelve and the early twenties. As it turns out, things aren't what we thought. What we do with our mind absolutely changes the structure and function of the brain. So why aren't we teaching our children and teens how to regulate their thoughts and brain? Research has proven that we can undoubtedly train and strengthen mind and the brain for the better – which results in a happier, healthier, and more resilient and loving human being.

In this Itty Bitty® Book you will find 15 simple things you can do to better understand what's going on in the hidden world of your teen. And more importantly, how to consciously train the brain and support their upward development from a mind, body, spirit perspective during this incredible stage of your child's life cycle.

You will learn the value, importance and tips for helping your teen strengthen the structure of their brain and regulate the mind.

Media and misaligned cultures have tragically perpetuated wrong and destructive beliefs about teens and adolescents. This book functions to coach parents into a greater understanding of the internal landscape of the teen so that we may better guide them into full expression of their potential, creativity and strength for becoming valuable contributors to our world.

They are not "problems," as myths would perpetuate. They are our solution to changing the landscape of our planet! Believe it or not, our children are higher humans than ourselves - and were meant to outstrip us in every way. They are here to usher in higher levels of peace, connectivity, cooperation, love and acceptance.

When we appropriately honor, respect and build them up from the inside out, they will step into the greater expression of who they are and who they were meant to become. Lack of motivation isn't their challenge. Rather it's immersing them in an environment that is void of meaningful contribution and that doesn't support how they think and feel.

Don't be surprised if improved relationships and a more harmonious family life is the resulting by-product of your efforts to change your understanding, language and perspective about your teen.

Let go of myths; open your mind and step into a space that is willing to understand the world and internal landscape of what a teen is experiencing. When you truly make this effort, you will meet your child with understanding, compassion and a fervent desire to lovingly guide them instead of resentfully reacting to them.

Strategy 1
Where Did My Kid Go?
Understanding the Great Brain Migration

The title is a metaphor that very accurately depicts the transformation occurring within the adolescent or teen brain. Adults would fall apart at the idea of going through such a transformation. The teen brain, on the other hand, is being hard-wired to survive and move through this incredible inner and outer human renovation process.

1. During adolescence and up through the early twenties, the brain (our internal hard drive) is completely transforming and overhauling itself – much like you would do with a computer... only it's a trillion times bigger task. Amazing!
2. Your teen, literally, doesn't have the same brain from one day to the next. Therefore, they may not be the same person from one moment to the next!
3. The brain is drastically pruning and building new circuitry. The reason they may not be able to focus is because the material simply ***isn't there*** or hasn't been rebuilt yet in a new and more useful way to support who they are becoming.
4. The above causes changes within the physical structure of the body and the way the mind thinks.
5. The mind influences the hard-wiring of the brain. The brain builds circuitry to match the level and quality of thought.

Parenting Tips

- Be gentle and understanding. They can't help how they feel. It's new to them too. They're far more confused than you are – *and* it's happening *to* them!
- Equip yourself with a better understanding for the critical ways your teen's brain and body are transforming and morphing them into something more.
- Believe in the idea that something ***incredible*** is happening to your teen – because it's true!
- Be encouraging. Remind them that struggles, emotions and feelings are temporary – and that they have the strength to get through the changes.
- Normalize things for your teen. On days when your teen is feeling focused, explain to them what's going on inside of them. Let them know that they may feel like a totally different person from one day to the next – *and it's NORMAL!*
- Choose words that lift and elevate your teen and support what they want, rather than using words that point out what's going wrong or not working. Choose words that strengthen instead of weaken.
- Teens don't know what to expect and they are biologically being driven to do more on their own or with their peers. Help them to feel good about these changes and value the transformation.

Strategy 2
Erasing the Misery of Myths

Now that you understand a little more about the function of adolescents, you may begin to see how the following myths are incorrect. In fact, they are blatantly harmful to the upward development of our young people. Hearing, thinking and believing the inaccurate thoughts and language that permeates from society, media and even within our own trusted families, greatly impacts the self-esteem, self-worth and confidence in teens, along with the ability to believe in themselves during this transformation. They have enough going on inside of them without having the world around them drag them down. Here are some of the myths and (on the next page) the real truth about what's going on during this life stage.

1. This is just a stage to "get through and get over with."
2. Teenage years are a period of immaturity and teens are trouble.
3. Teens are unmotivated.
4. Their hormones are running wild.

The Real Truth

- This is an important stage in between being a child and operating with an adult mind and body. Teens need support and guidance to help them build a brain and mind that is resilient, regulated and stable. Your child has a unique purpose for being here, and ensuring that they are strong, loving, capable and full of self-awareness is critical for positive reconstruction of their brain and the quality of thought generated by the mind.
- Teens aren't trouble, nor are their transformation processes immature. It's one of the most incredible complex feats of nature! Teens need healthy outlets for their creative surges and newly forming expressions of their new self. Their brains crave novelty and many learning environments are often putting their brains to sleep and lowering dopamine levels (see chapter 7).
- Teens have a new and improved way of viewing life and the world. They simply care about different things *differently* than the previous generations. Generally they aren't unmotivated, just disenchanted with adults' resistance to change and better ways of thinking, doing, being and learning.
- Hormones aren't running wild. Sex hormones are simply increasing. Changes in behavior are due to changes in the structure and function of the brain.

Strategy 3
Words – The Weapon of The Wise

When you change the language, you can change the teen. Teens respond to our words. Society has allowed itself to use ill-fitted and ill-fated words to describe teens and adolescents.

1. Use words and thoughts that come from a place of wisdom, understanding and a reverence for your child's transformation process. In doing so, you fortify your child from within in immeasurable ways.
2. Release fear-based thoughts and words – forever! These are the most harmful and destructive patterns that exist within human consciousness. They originate in childhood and get encoded into our genetics and subconscious.
3. Choose words that lift and elevate your teen's perspective and thinking.
4. Commit to **refusing** to think or say negative beliefs about your teen such as: they won't make it; they're a mess or mixed up; or they're always hanging out with the wrong crowd.
5. The Law of Attraction is always in operation and you either project life affirming or harmful energy and manifestations upon your child by the quality of thoughts and words that you choose to launch.
6. Tone talks! Observe the tone and meaning behind your words. Ensure they're emanating wisdom and grace.

Helpful Tips 2

They may not act like it, but your teen hears more than you think. They are listening! Here are some tips to help you choose your words wisely.

- Always speak with the grace of a benevolent queen (mom) or king (dad) – even if you don't feel like it. You're demonstrating how to do it, and that they too are capable of regulating their own words and behaviors. Priceless parenting!
- Use words that build momentum for what you want. Eliminate language and thoughts about the things you don't like. Your words either feed or starve positive or negative manifestational outcomes for your teen and you. Choose wisely!
- Use words that communicate their value, worthiness and importance for being here…and of their life!
- Remember, you are teaching them how to (beneficially) change the function and structure of the brain via regulating how the mind thinks and the quality of its thoughts and consequentially-produced emotions.
- Use authentic, caring and loving words and tones. You can still be firm (when you need to) and loving at the same time.
- Attach authentic, kind emotion and feelings to your words and wisdom. Your teen will feel the difference. Teens love authenticity!

Strategy 4
Leave Me Alone!

Next time your adolescent or teen utters these words, rather than taking it personally, reflect and go deeper into the inner meaning of their words. Teens are trying to prepare themselves for doing, living and being mostly on their own. They have to learn to work through struggles, challenges, experiences and relationships with greater independence. Here's what they may be trying to achieve and communicate through this statement.

1. I need to survive and thrive on my own. Or at least I need to *think* I'm doing this on my own. Please believe in me!
2. Any productive things you can do to release the mental struggle would be great, and since this isn't happening, the best thing from my perspective would be to get out of my hair. I need constructive words that make me feel better about myself or the situation, not worse!
3. I desperately want to know that you love and approve of me – even when I don't have everything all figured out and I mess up.
4. I'm craving independence; I need you to nourish it in healthy ways.
5. Intuitively I DO know that "feeling good" is ideal. And when you're angry and yelling at me, you're out of alignment. So get out, because you clearly don't know how to help the situation any better than me.

Helpful Coaching Tips

Even though your adolescent/teen's behavior is telling you one thing, physically and emotionally they really may want another. Be a patient, loving guide that assists them in making sense of their struggles.

- Be the parent who can demonstrate "**how**" to act when things are going chaotic. Don't provide wisdom that you're not willing to demonstrate. Teens despise when adults do this – and they stop listening and valuing your parenting. Therefore, using words like "because I said so," doesn't cut it!
- Let them know that you appreciate them for trying to navigate life more on their own and that they always have a safety net (home and you), should things get too confusing, challenging or if they're in need of some refueling and help.
- Teach them that asking for help is a ***strength,*** not a weakness! Demonstrate how to ask for help while still being self-reliant, resourceful and responsible.
- Use helpful, kind language and tones, while releasing ***all*** judgmental and guilting statements. Your teen is learning and you're providing a safe training ground for doing so. This *is* the function and responsibility of a *home*.

Strategy 5
There's a New Family in Town – Peers

Get used to it! It is the way it is suppose to be. You are being replaced for an important reason. Nature is making it possible for them to have the courage to go out on their own and be able to handle different kinds of personalities and experiences without falling apart. If you try to thwart this process, you debilitate their mind, body, and spiritual growth and development.

1. The limbic system of the brain is changing, saying "Go with peers and not your parents." Peer relationships are like life and death to a teen's functioning.
2. Let go of fear. This doesn't mean you stop ensuring their safety. Rather, you're shifting your consciousness into more constructive territory and strategies.
3. Ensure that your teen understands the importance of maintaining a healthy balance of family and peer activities. Teach them that both can be a part of their life. Let them know it's great to hang out with their friends, and to also contribute to the family in meaningful ways (e.g., eating dinner at home; adding to discussions at the dinner table; family outings; maintaining responsibilities).
4. Be flexible. It's not a 50/50 deal. In fact, it's normal for them to spend a majority of time with friends.

Helpful Coaching Tips.

- Don't be offended by your teen's lack of interest in hanging out with you like they use to. Biologically, they're being driven to branch out into the gene pool. If not, they'd be marrying their cousins. So feel gratitude that they're going in the right direction!
- It's not about you. Take your emotions out of it and focus on giving wise and benevolent guidance instead of punishment to your child. This is what they need most.
- Love and accept them for who they are and who they are becoming. They are not you and are not supposed to think the way you do. More often than not, they are our superiors - with highly evolved thinking and emotions.
- Do not guilt your teen. Making them responsible for your emotional feelings is not their responsibility – it's yours! You can still teach them to be compassionate human beings without being responsible for another's lack of management over their own emotional set-points. Be able to demonstrate this. When you do so, you will be fortifying them for a lifetime and preventing them from being a victim of anything and anyone – including peers!
- Fortify your child early with healthy inner (self) and outer (family/friends) connections, which will help to greatly avoid unhealthy peer/dating relationships.

Strategy 6
You Are Not Your Emotions

From the full perspective of your total human construct (of mind, body and spirit), emotions are simply a technology and an internal guidance system. So often people *think* they are what their emotions are telling them. This couldn't be further from the truth! Here's what emotions do and are *telling* you when you listen and apply.

1. Help you determine how far off or how correctly aligned you are with the perspective of your highest Inner Self (Soul, Higher Self, Spirit, etc.). The better you feel, the greater the alignment.
2. If you are authentically feeling the highest of human emotions (love, joy, gratitude, inspiration, compassion, peace, forgiveness, faith, etc.) you are completely and perfectly aligned with your Higher Self's perspective.
3. If you are feeling the lower levels on the guidance system (fear, worry, guilt, blame, victimization, powerlessness, anger, etc.), your thoughts and perspective are operating from the ego instead of your Higher Self on the subject, person or experience at hand.
4. Emotions *assist* you in navigating life's experiences with greater stability, clarity and effectiveness.

*For a complete emotional scale (22 incremental emotions), google Abraham-Hicks Emotional Guidance Scale.

What You Can Do

Here are a few conscious parenting tips for managing emotions.

- Get rid of fear-based thinking. Thoughts have vibrations and quantum physics is proving that we create realities through our thoughts!
- Select upward thoughts and emotions.
- Invest wisely in what you choose to think, say and believe about your child's situation and abilities.
- Lighten up and don't take yourself so seriously! Do your best to add humor and levity to life's circumstances and experiences. Kids love anything silly and fun. A joyful brain/mind is an integrated and resilient brain/mind!
- Use proper discernment and common sense. There are times when real fear is an appropriate response. Too often, however, we create fearful reactions and stress. Stress is harmful and corrosive to the mind and physical body.

Conscious Parenting Statements
- "You are not your emotions. They are only a technology for you to use."
- "Help me understand how you feel so that I can better support you."
- "The way you are behaving isn't okay. We all have to work together. You may come out of your room when you are feeling yourself again."

Strategy 7
Novelty! Novelty! Novelty!

Dopamine is a neurochemical that has an important effect upon the teenage brain and affects how they think, feel and act. If you want to understand your teen, tune into their lives and consequential levels of dopamine production. It will tell you a lot about where they are mentally, emotionally, spiritually and how they physically might act. Dopamine is responsible for creative inspirations and meaning. Here's the dopamine download.

1. Produces pleasure or thrill feelings. It's released from the brain when we feel novelty, inspiration or feel like we did something good.
2. Teens can experience strong surges in dopamine levels. Just because levels are high doesn't mean they produce higher baseline levels! In fact, baseline levels often drop lower in teens and adolescents. Take notice!
3. Baseline dopamine levels = boredom. Boredom feels horrible to the novelty seeking creative teen brain and mind!
4. Novelty releases a big spurt of dopamine so that teens are driven to experience new adventures like creating new things or leaving the safety and familiarity of family to hang out with unpredictable peers.
5. What's the downside of misguidance and poor regulation? Addiction. Every addiction is driven by dopamine (gambling, video games, shopping, alcohol or other).

Things You Can Do

- Talk to your teen about dopamine, including what it does, how it works, and to recognize the up and down sides of it and suggestions for management.
- Notice when your teen acts or tells you that they're bored – especially for extended periods of time or increased frequency. Time to step in!
- Liven things up in your family life by creating novel things to do. Let your children come up with healthy novel ideas (both individually and as a family).
- Help them to feel good about themselves.
- Honor their interests and ideas. Listen carefully to the real "needs" behind the request or idea. Some might need greater independence, a need to travel, to create something, help others, etc.
- Avoid addiction and excessive thrill-seeking behaviors by fortifying your child from within and from without, through healthy outlets that are of interest and meaningful to them!
- Be responsive to counterproductive behaviors that impede the teen brain, mind and dopamine production such as:
    - Excessive testing and memorization.
    - Stressing them out unnecessarily.
    - Taking away (healthy) novelty.
    - Teaching them to compete aggressively against each other.
    - Imply or say they're a mess after we've imposed the above items upon them.

Strategy 8
From Limitations to Limitlessness

Adolescence is a period of great potential and constructive power. The constructive side of this time period has led our world into many incredible innovations. If they are to reach their full human potential, we must look at them from the highest and most respected vantage point. Characteristics of adolescents:

1. Time of expansion and enormous creativity. Ensure that it is nourished!
2. An age that leads society into new and higher states of mass consciousness, emotions and methods of operating collectively with one another.
3. Pushes away from traditional ways of thinking and doing things and expands our out-of-the-box thinking.
4. Pushes against systems and explores new solutions to world problems and paradigms.
5. Adults seek to keep things the same, while adolescents are driven to create new ideas, ways of being and doing. Teens want change and aren't interested in the status quo! And adults don't want their boat rocked. This is what leads to stagnation in adults and the friction that often occurs between parents and their teens. (*Note: From a spiritual perspective, continuous learning and transformation is the secret ingredient to youth and staying young!*)

How To Support Your Teen

Get acquainted with your teen's purpose and their reason for being here as a contributing member of humanity. They are greatly needed!

- Remind your teen often that they are very important to the world's plan of peace and upward development. This builds their value and self-worth – and, helps them release good-feeling brain chemicals!
- Remind them also of their skills, good qualities and attributes, instead of spending extra energy and time discussing what they aren't good at. The latter stresses them out and the former builds positive circuitry within the brain.
- Find out what inspires them or what excites their passions and interests.
- What do they love doing that they get lost in, or lose track of time?
- What personal attributes or gifts do they have to share with the world? Are they funny, sensitive, forgiving, accepting, a convener, a supporter, musical or loving toward the environment and life?
- Help them find ways to exercise and build what they're good at and what they enjoy doing – even if it isn't what you value or think won't make them money. Their Soul will find ways to use the gifts they were intended to share.

Strategy 9
Building Mindful Awareness

Your mind is the virtual (non-physical) part of you that can generate thoughts and reasoning that shapes your reality about yourself, your experiences, relationships and your emotional responses. Mindful awareness is a state of being aware of your own mind and what it's thinking from moment-to-moment.

1. You and your life are a product of what you are thinking, whether it's mindfully or mindlessly. When your thoughts are aligned to your Higher Self, you can actually observe yourself thinking – and then redirect your mind to higher thoughts that are shaped in love, acceptance, gratitude, peace, etc.
2. Both mind and brain are transforming at incredible rates during adolescence.
3. You can use the mind to change the function and structure of the brain – for better or worse!

Teach your child/teen to slow down, quiet, empty and regulate the mind through the following:

1. Learn to interrupt your rambling thoughts.
2. Become the "observer" of your thoughts and redirect the mind by taking several deep breaths and choosing new and improved thoughts and emotions.
3. Stay in the present moment! Ignore racing thoughts of the past or future.

Characteristics of an Unregulated Mind or Mindlessness

- Races with thoughts or anxiety.
- Is in a state of chatter, noise, reactivity and chaos and has challenges focussing.
- Frequently worries and stresses.
- Laments and/or stresses about the past or the future or plays scenarios over and over in the mind.
- Is full, bombarded and has difficulty handling additional life experiences.
- Is paranoid or superstitious.
- Resides in drama cycles – either starting drama, keeping it going or desires a diet of drama (from TV or other sources).
- Is fearful or engaged in lower emotional levels of thinking.

Regulated Mind or Mindful Awareness

- Wise, calm, peaceful and full of clarity.
- Integrated brain and mind is resilient.
- Elevates dopamine levels – naturally!
- Empty, uncluttered and open to ideas, possibilities and intuitive downloads.
- Creative, inspired and stable.
- Easily holds higher levels of thoughts and is a creative problem solver.
- Calmly vigilant and alert, free of worry.
- Able to listen to the direction of the Soul.

Teach your teen to spend their energy shaping their thoughts for the better. Better brain = healthier happier body and emotions!

Strategy 10
Mind-Body Alignment

One of the most important, yet neglected areas of parenting is teaching kids mind-body connection and alignment. Your mind and emotional states are highly influenced by the health of the physical body, rest and the foods that you put into it. A healthy vibrant body also is more receptive to receiving and growing spiritual intuition. The following can cause a person to feel *off*, emotional or unbalanced:

1. Eating low quality foods.
2. Lack of physical activity.
3. Lack of sleep.
4. Too much stress or screen time.
5. Not engaged in meaningful, inspiring work or activities – i.e., not feeling a sense of purpose.

The Brain

1. When your physical and mental systems are balanced, peaceful and appropriately nourished, your body is capable of great feats of healing, stability, regeneration, repair and longevity.
2. Science is proving that you have the ability to either express or suppress harmful or beneficial genes based upon the quality of what you think, feel and how you nourish your physical body.

How to Balance the Body & Mind

- Your physical body works really hard for you. Teach kids to love and have reverence for their body instead of criticizing it. Each cell within our body responds favorably to love and gratitude!
- Eat fresh, organic, high quality unprocessed foods from nature as much as possible.
- Sleep and rest your body when it's tired.
- Drink natural spring or higher quality waters, in place of municipal water whenever possible (which is high in chlorine and other harmful chemicals).
- Eat lots of dark green and leafy vegetables.
- Eat a variety (and colors) of plant-based vegetables and fruits.
- Include high quality oils in the diet – fish, Omega 3 and 6 oils.

Avoid low frequency and low quality foods that interfere with exceptional vibrancy and functioning of your body and brain. These include:

- Sugar, preservatives, chemical flavorings/dyes, sodas, juice drinks
- Stimulants – caffeine drinks, energy drinks, coffees, etc.
- Sports drinks (e.g., Gatorade, PowerAde)
- Minimize wheat products and other high gluten products. Substitute quinoa or whole grain rice.
- Minimize dairy (cow) products.

Strategy 11
Discipline Done Right

There will be times when it's necessary to teach teens that there are consequences to their actions. Knowing the differences between discipline and punishment will help you guide your teen more effectively, while preserving your relationship with one another.

Punishment operates on the low end of the emotional scale and does the following:

1. Has the intention of hurting or causing pain.
2. Teaches children to fear and resent the parent or the punisher.
3. Teaches children how to motivate or bully by fear.
4. Teaches children that punishing others is an acceptable way to operate and motivate others or themselves.
5. Teaches children to use physical, psychological and emotional tactics for punishing others in order to get their way or get a person to do what they want.
6. Teaches children to dominate another human being or life form.
7. Trains kids to be deceptive about their actions so that they don't get caught.
8. Promotes a fear-based approach resulting in lower self-esteem, self-worth and power and control struggles.

Discipline – Upward Parenting Strategy

- The goal of discipline is to help teens learn self-discipline, which allows kids to engage in an experience and learn *from it*. If you don't teach your children to acquire self-discipline, they are likely to experience greater challenges as they attempt to regulate themselves in life.
- Removing their ability to regulate their mind and actions (or worse, bypassing the lesson altogether), is like stripping a human being of their foundation, which can result in poor relationships, drug use or risky behaviors.
- Discipline shows them that there are consequences to their actions and that they are accountable to regulate their mind, emotions and desires.
- Discipline operates on the high end of the emotional scale and keeps in tact, dignity, value, self-worth and respect for everyone involved.
- Helps build a child's internal compass for empathy, kindness, love and peace.
- Invites and expects cooperation within the family. The purpose of a family is to teach and demonstrate that people can work together and support each other despite differences.
- Sets limits with choices. Like adults, kids want to feel they have some control over their life. Kids can be offered choices within the limits set by the parent.

Strategy 12
Leveraging Your "Wrongs"

You want a sure-fire way to get the attention of your teen? Admit you've made a mistake – especially when your teen was right! Below are a few common comments that you will hear coming from teens. Take a deep soulful look at each and the message behind them...and discern if there isn't a strong element of truth that you personally, or the environment, needs to fix.

1. I hate school.
2. You need to relax.
3. You don't know how I feel.
4. It doesn't matter (i.e., taking tests, what someone said or did, when adults want kids to get angry at political issues, etc.)
5. No I don't want to think and talk about it. (When a parent rehashes all the things that went wrong or was said wrongly.)
6. You (mom, dad) don't know. (Translation: you can't feel it, understand it, or don't know as much as you think you do about how I feel on the subject.)

Each generation is meant to evolve past the previous. Take a deep look at the qualities and characteristics of the current young generation. There you will find the secrets to advancing your own evolution, while supporting teens with the important transformations that they came here to make for all of us.

Correcting Errors

Upward parenting requires that you learn to fully regulate your own mind, body and emotions and be able to change unwanted beliefs and mental programs. Remember, your teen may not have the old stubborn deep-seated fears and beliefs that you have or grew up with. However, if they do and you're able to come into awareness about how you incorrectly advised them, say so! Here's some safe helpful language and examples to use with your teen.

- "You know kiddo, I never learned how to use the emotional scale. It's not my parents fault because no one taught it to them either. But now that I do know, I want to show you how useful and powerful it can be."
- "As a parent, I'm always learning. All of us are...and should always strive to keep evolving our thoughts, behaviors and emotions to higher levels. I recently learned something...I've been teaching and demonstrating the wrong thing to you – and I'm very sorry."
- (Continued from bullet #2) "The good news is, we aren't a victim of anything or anyone and we *can* change how we think, feel, what we do and our emotions at anytime. All we have to do is give our ***attention*** and ***focus*** to doing so. May I show you the new way and how it helped me?"
- "I'm so grateful that you opened up my perspective and thinking. You are right. Let's work through this constructively."

Strategy 13
Banishing Beliefs

If you or your teen have mostly beneficial belief patterns – wonderful! Nurture and nourish them well. The ones that don't serve you are the ones you want to shift. Here's how it works.

1. A belief isn't real. It's only a thought you keep thinking long enough until it feels like truth or it feels real to you. (i.e., I'm ugly, not a happy person, not good enough, can't do ___, nobody likes me, my parents and teachers hate me, etc.)
2. Most beliefs and thought patterns get hardwired into our brains between 0-7 years. These thought patterns get stored in an area of the brain that makes them "automatic" (you don't think about them, they just happen, e.g., you don't relearn to walk and talk everyday – it just happens). Beliefs become automatic in the same way. Most beliefs originate in childhood from programs our parents gave us.
3. Beliefs can be changed at any time. This means you can rewire the hard-drive of your brain any time. This is the *golden key* to a happy life.
    a. You just have to be mindful and aware of what you are thinking and believing and then,
    b. You have to **want** to change your thoughts about it. Remember, we create with our minds!

Steps to Uprooting Unwanted Beliefs

- Awareness – nonjudgmentally examine the beliefs you have about yourself, a situation, person, emotion, etc.
- Open your point of view. Look at the "thing" from other vantage points. Look at the bright side instead of the dark side. Take a forgiving and releasing approach – i.e., let it go!
- Say (out loud) affirmations that support item #2. (See examples below.)
- Visualize the desired outcome/scenario for yourself or the situation.
- Fully immerse yourself in the feeling of bullet #4 and imagine as if the good outcome already happened and you're living in its results. This means, even though you don't see the evidence of it in your physical reality, live as though it has already happened!
- Feel gratitude that this belief has dissolved for everyone's highest good.
- Then sit back, relax and notice how life shifts its course for you (as you stay committed to this new thought pattern).

Things you can say:

- I AM willing to release old beliefs now. They have no hold over me.
- I AM wise and willing to look at this in a different way that benefits others and me.
- It makes me feel great to let go of this old belief. I don't need it and it doesn't need me! I AM free now!

Strategy 14
Selective Parenting

Nothing will sabotage your hard work and progress faster than operating in the "selective parenting" mode. Selective parenting is similar to selective listening – choosing to engage when it's convenient. Well-intentioned parents are often committed to their kids by ensuring outcomes, positive discipline and by participating in their lives in meaningful ways. However, too often, parents will choose their own distractions and fun instead of "hanging in there" when it gets inconvenient. Scenario example:

1. Your teen is having substance abuse challenges and is grounded.
2. You've been holding strong with supervision for quite some time and then you get invited to an incredible event, party or on an exciting date.
3. Rather than committing to your teen by staying home/supervising, you go out.

This is selective parenting and it communicates:
1. My parent's fun is more important than their commitment to my (teen's) welfare. And, if you (mom/dad) aren't committed to my outcome and well-being, why should I be? I'll model you. And I will be tempted – just like you are now.
2. You don't mean what you say.
3. My well-being isn't the most important thing and I'm not a top priority.

Things You Can Do to Ensure Higher Outcomes.

- Be honest about yourself, parenting attitudes and selective parenting.
- Notice the quality and quantity of attention you give to your teen and when.
- Find out what is important *to them*.
- Instead of feeling guilty about your mistakes, spend that energy and time engaging with your #1 priority – your child!

When you make sacrifices for your child and temporarily give up personal opportunities to ensure that they receive the necessary supervision/attention, use conscious language such as the following to help your teen understand their value and self-worth. Never guilt them for your sacrifices!

- "I choose to be here with you because you are far more important to me than going to any event."
- "I will never give up on you. I know you can accomplish anything you want - but you are going to learn to do it the right way."
- "Ensuring that you grow up into a happy, healthy, resilient and loving person is the most important thing to me."
- "I know you're capable of getting yourself back on track. Sometimes it's challenging to do it on your own. You'll be there in no time. So stick with it and keep going. You're stronger than you think!"

Strategy 15
The Happiness Factor

The human brain functions best when it is happy. This is especially true for teens. Science has unequivocally proven that a happy brain works better! A happy brain and mind:

1. Is more integrated = increased electrical communication between the various hemispheres resulting in better decision making and reflection
2. More creative
3. More resilient
4. More intuitive and can receive clearer messaging from the Higher Self (Superconsciousness or Soul)
5. Manifests at higher levels
6. Is more mindfully aware
7. Helps to release positive feeling neurotransmitters and hormones so that we feel stable, motivated and inspired by life
8. Produces healing effects within the body and improved immune function
9. Reduces stress and anxiety
10. Creates improved sleep cycles
11. Can positively impact genetics and suppress harmful gene expression
12. Fosters feelings of gratitude, which has positive effects on the brain, mind emotions and so much more!

Coaching Tips & Strategies

- Pay attention to adults, coaches and teachers who are leading and guiding your children with fear-based, punishing language and tactics.
- Use the above as an opportunity to chat with your teen about how to effectively navigate people or areas of their life and environment that still perpetuate old paradigms of thinking and being that are destructive to how their brain, body and mind function best.
- Help them understand that they are in charge of what they think and feel. You own your mind and nobody has the ability to take it from you - unless you give it away. Therefore, what your teen thinks about him/herself is the most important thing! Not what others say *about* them.
- Participate in activities that calm, relax and elevate happiness and consciousness within the mind and body such as: meditation; physical exercise; laugh and smile as much as you possibly can; express gratitude for all things great and small; try something new; practice daily giving and receiving; practice one altruistic act daily. The Internet is a great resource for finding exercises for each area.
- Practice gratitude exercises daily or when feeling down. Gratitude immediately lifts the emotions, brain function and stimulates good-feeling hormones. As you advance, practice being grateful for the tough or less desirable situations. Find the silver lining and your inner world will reap the rewards!

You've finished. Before you go…

Tweet/share that you finished this book.

Please star rate this book.

Reviews are solid gold to writers. Please take a few minutes to give us some itty bitty feedback on this book and post it on line.

ABOUT THE AUTHOR

Gretchen is a Children's Health Innovation and Program Prevention Specialist, a Conscious Parenting Expert and the Founder of Mind Body Spirit Parenting. As a 25-year veteran in the areas of applied neuroscience, behavioral nutrition, substance abuse, eating disorders, physiology, physical/emotional/social school health and conscious parenting, Gretchen creates a multifaceted holistic approach to affect change in paradigms for children and parents by teaching people how to utilize their human technologies of mind, body and spirit to improve every aspect of life, health and the human experience.

Gretchen is an author, human potential expert and has spoken locally and nationally on children and adult health topics. Her programs have been featured in the LA Times, Parent Magazine, on Los Angeles area news channels, Blue Zones Project, IDEA and her school health initiatives have received national recognition from the Alliance for a Healthier Generation.

For more information about Gretchen, conscious parenting topics or to obtain a copy of a comprehensive lifetime parenting guidebook ("Mind Body Spirit Parenting Guidebook – Developing The Conscious Child"), visit:

www.thekidwhisper.com

**If You Liked This Book
You Might Also Enjoy…**

- **Your Amazing Itty Bitty® Family Leadership Book** – Jacqueline T.D. Huynh

- **Your Amazing Itty Bitty® Communicating With Your Teenager Book** – Christine Alisa, MS

- **Your Amazing Itty Bitty® Weight Loss Book** – Suzy Prudden and Joan Meijer-Hirschland

With many more Amazing Itty Bitty® Books available in paperback and online…

www.ingramcontent.com/pod-product-compliance
Lightning Source LLC
Chambersburg PA
CBHW061304040426
42444CB00010B/2517